JOURNAL

OF THE

STATE CONVENTION

OF

SOUTH CAROLINA;

TOGETHER WITH THE

RESOLUTION AND ORDINANCE.

PRINTED BY ORDER OF THE CONVENTION.

COLUMBIA, S. C.:
JOHNSTON & CAVIS, PRINTERS TO THE CONVENTION.

1852

In Convention, Friday, April 30, 1852.

Ordered, That five thousand copies of the proceedings of this Convention, and of the Report, Resolution, and Ordinance, be printed; and that the same be distributed as follows, under the superintendence of the Clerk:

For the Executive, three hundred copies; for each of our Senators and Representatives in Congress, for their own use, one hundred copies; for each member of this Convention, and of the State Legislature, ten copies; and that the remaining copies be for public distribution.

JOURNAL

OF THE

STATE CONVENTION.

MONDAY, APRIL 26, 1852.

Pursuant to an act of the Legislature of the State of South Carolina, entitled "An act to provide for the appointment of Deputies to a Southern Congress, and to call a Convention of the People of this State,"* ratified on 20th day of December, 1850; and also "An act to fix the time for the meeting of the Convention elected under the authority of an act entitled 'An act to provide for the appointment of Delegates to a Southern Congress, and to call a Convention of the people of this State,'" passed in the year of our Lord one thousand eight hundred and fifty, ratified on the 16th December, 1851, the Delegates of the several election districts and parishes of this State assembled in the Hall of the House of Representatives, in the Capitol, at Columbia, in the State of South Carolina, on this day, at 12 o'clock, meridian.

On motion of Mr. EDMUND BELLINGER, jr., a Delegate from Barnwell, the Hon. David L. Wardlaw, a Delegate from Abbeville, was called to the Chair, and Mr. Richard J. Davant, a Delegate from St. Lukes, was requested to act as Secretary.

The Convention having been called to order, the Election Districts and Parishes were called over, whereupon the following Delegates appeared at the Clerk's desk, presented their credentials, and enrolled their names:

Abbeville.

D. L. WARDLAW,
THOS. C. PERRIN,
J. C. MARTIN,
GEO. W. PRESSLY.
G. R. McCALLA.

---

* See Addenda, at the end of the Journal.

All Saints'.

T. PINCKNEY ALSTON,
PETER VAUGHT.

Barnwell.

E. BELLINGER, jr.,
S. W. TROTTI,
A. P. ALDRICH,
J. V. MARTIN,
WINCHESTER GRAHAM.

Chester.

SAML. McALILEY,
C. T. SCAIFE,
I. MOBLEY,
WM. A. ROSBOROUGH.

Chesterfield.

J. C. COIT,
W. J. HANNA,
HUGH CRAIG.

Christ Church.

JACOB BOND I'ON,
A. V. TOOMER.

Claremont.

W. HAYNSWORTH,
THOS. R. ENGLISH, sr.,
F. SUMTER.
A. C. SPAIN.

Clarendon.

JOHN P. RICHARDSON.

Darlington.

JOSIAH J. EVANS,
E. W. CHARLES,
E. A. LAW,

Edgefield.

JAMES JONES,
F. H. WARDLAW,
F. W. PICKENS,
M. L. BONHAM,
R. B. BOUKNIGHT,
WILEY HARRISON.

Fairfield.

JOHN H. MEANS,
WM. A. OWENS,
JOHN BUCHANAN.

Greenville.

B. F. PERRY,
THOS. P. BROCKMAN,
VARDRY McBEE,
JESSE CENTER,
P. E. DUNCAN.

Horry.

HARTFORD JONES.

Kershaw.

JOHN CANTEY,
THOS. LANG,
L. J. PATTERSON.

Lancaster.

JOHN WILLIAMS,
JAMES D. McILWAIN.

Laurens.

H. C. YOUNG,
A. C. JONES,
THOMAS WRIGHT,
JOHN D. WILLIAMS,
J. H. IRBY.

Lexington.

H. J. CAUGHMAN,
HENRY ARTHUR,
JOHN C. HOPE.

Marion.

W. W. HARLLEE,
WILLIAM EVANS,
JOHN C. BETHEA,
W. R. JOHNSON.

Marlboro'.

JAMES E. DAVID,
WM. J. COOK,
WM. T. ELLERBE.

Newberry.

F. B. HIGGINS,
J. H. WILLIAMS,
PETER MOON,
DRAYTON NANCE

Orange Parish.

D. F. JAMISON,
M. GRAMLING.

Pendleton.

F. BURT,
JOHN MAXWELL,
JOHN MARTIN,
J. N. WHITNER,
R. A. MAXWELL,
F. W. SYMMES.

Prince William's.

B. McBRIDE,
G. C. MACKAY.
JOHN E. FRAMPTON,

Prince George, Winyaw.

J. HARLESTON READ,
J. H. TRAPIER,
BENJ. H. WILSON,
SAMUEL T. ATKINSON.

Richland.

W. F. DeSAUSSURE,
J. U. ADAMS,
A. H. GLADDEN,
MAXCY GREGG,
C. BOOKTER.

Spartanburg.

JOHN G. LANDRUM,
JAS. FARROW,
J. WINSMITH,
P. M. WALLACE,
R. C. POOLE.

St. Andrew's.

JOHN RIVERS,
ALEXANDER H. BROWN.

St. Bartholomew's.

E. St. P. BELLINGER, DAVID WALKER,
LEWIS O'BRYAN, D. S. HENDERSON.

St. George's, Dorchester.

I. M. DWIGHT.

St. Helena.

EDMD. RHETT, JOHN FRIPP.

St. James', Goose Creek.

ISAAC BRADWELL, jr., WEST WILLIAMS.

St. James', Santee.

DANL. DuPRE, SAML. J. PALMER.

St. John's, Berkley.

MORTON WARING, PHILIP C. KIRK.

St. John's, Colleton.

W. B. SEABROOK, E. M. WHALEY
HUGH WILSON, jr.,

St. Luke's.

JULIUS G. HUGUENIN, R. J. DAVANT.

St. Mathew's.

O. M. DANTZLER, H. A. HAIGLER.

St. Paul's.

J. BERKLEY GRIMBALL, E. B. SCOTT.

St. Peter's.

D. H. HAMILTON,
A. M. RUTH,
E. MARTIN

St. Philips and St. Michael's.

LANGDON CHEVES.
A. P. BUTLER,
EDWD. FROST,
C. M. FURMAN,
DANL. E. HUGER,
M. KING,
R. W. BARNWELL,
BENJ. F. DUNKIN,
W. PERONNEAU FINLEY,
THOS. LEHRE,
CHAS. MACBETH,
I. W. HAYNE,
JOHN BELLINGER,
A. G. MAGRATH,
EWD. McCRADY,
JOHN CUNINGHAM.

St. Stephen's.

W. MAZYCK PORCHER,
T. L. GOURDIN,

St. Thomas and St. Dennis.

GEO. ELFE.

Union.

J. S. SIMS,
WM. J. BOBO,
B. H. RICE,
J. M. GADBERRY.

Williamsburg.

D. M. MASON,
S. E. GRAHAM.

York.

R. Y. RUSSEL,
ROBT. T. ALLISON,
W. A. LATTA.

One hundred and forty-nine delegates having appeared, the presiding officer announced that a quorum was present; whereupon the Convention proceeded with its organization.

The Convention proceeded to the election of President, and, upon an inspection of the ballots, it appeared that his Excellency JOHN H. MEANS, Governor and Commander-in-Chief in and over the State of South Carolina, a delegate in this Convention from the District of Fairfield, had been chosen.

On motion of the Hon. JACOB BOND I'ON, a delegate from Christ Church Parish, a committee of three was appointed to wait on his Excellency the Governor, to inform him of his election and conduct him to the chair; and it was ordered that the Convention do rise and be uncovered to receive the President.

Messrs. CANTEY, DESAUSSURE, and OWENS, were appointed the committee, who immediately conducted his Excellency the Governor to the chair, who proceeded to address the Convention as follows:

Gentlemen of the Convention:

Although I am fully aware that I am indebted more to my official station than to any merit of my own for the distinguished honor you have conferred upon me, yet I must be permitted to express my profound gratitude to you for having honored that station in my person. Unaccustomed as I am to parliamentary usages, I should be disposed to shrink from the position you have assigned me, but that I feel assured that I will be sustained and assisted in the discharge of its duties by the same kindness which has prompted you to bestow it upon me. While I am fully alive to its responsibilities, I trust I feel still deeper the solemn responsibility which rests upon me as a member of this Convention. We have met together clothed in the sovereign power of the land. The voice of this Convention, when it speaks, must be potential for good or for evil. How much prudence, how much caution and deliberation, does it become us to use before we act! It is useless for me to enter into a detail of the peculiar circumstances under which we have met; a mere allusion to them is sufficient to bring to your minds the fact that they are full of embarrassment. We certainly have a most delicate part to act—one which we cannot perform with credit to ourselves, or with honor to the State, unless we are buoyed by a devoted patriotism above the petty considerations of party strife, of personal ambition, or which is even worse and more to be deprecated, vindictive feelings to each other because we differ in opinion. The external circumstances by which we are surrounded fearfully admonish us that we have no strength to waste in internal feuds. The very dangers of our position call loudly upon us to be united. But, unfortunately for us and the great cause of the South, we are not united. We have been divided and distracted by the convulsive throes of party strife. The great question of our wrongs has been forgotten amid our wranglings as to the remedy.

While this state of things exists among us, the fiendish fanaticism of an abolition spirit, which tramples all law, both human and divine, under foot, is steadily moving forward towards the accomplishment of its ends. If we intend not basely to desert the cause in which we have been so long engaged, and finally submit to our degradation and ruin, this tide of fanaticism must be sooner or later met. As dark as are the dangers which surround us, still more gloomy are those which threaten us from our internal commotions. If we are united, we need fear no danger. The justice of our cause, and our strong arms, will be sufficient to protect us. But if, in the madness of party strife, we fall upon each other and forget the common enemy, an easy victory will be accomplished by them; a victory which will bring ruin and disgrace upon us. The very first object of this Convention should be to heal these divisions. I will not presume to suggest the course which will be proper for you to pursue to accomplish this great object, and to maintain the honor and dignity of our beloved State. This must be a matter of consultation and deliberation. The intelligence, the patriotism, the dignity of this body, are an earnest that that course will be one which will involve no *sacrifice* of *principle;* one, the object of which will be to promote the best interests of our State. We meet together as members of one common family, whose interest, honor, and destiny are the same. A deep devotion to our country and its institutions should be the polar star to guide us in our course. The arm of our State, which was recently strong and ready to strike, has been paralyzed alone by our dissensions. Let us heal them at once, that with firm and united strength we may meet the enemies of our institutions. Upon *the union* of our State, I solemnly believe, depends our *destiny.*

Mr. DESAUSSURE moved that the proceedings of the Convention be opened with prayer, and that the Rev. J. C. COIT, a delegate from Chesterfield, be requested to officiate at this time; which was agreed to, and the proceedings were opened with prayer accordingly.

Mr. EDMUND BELLINGER, jr., offered the following Resolution; which was agreed to:

Resolved, That the Assistant Clerk of the House of Representatives be requested to furnish stationery, to be placed on the tables of the members of the Convention, from what he has in the possession of the House of Representatives.

The Convention proceeded to the election of Clerk.

Hon. JACOB BOND I'ON nominated JAMES A. STROBHART as a candidate for the office.

Whereupon the Convention proceeded to a ballot, and the Chair appointed Messrs. CUNINGHAM, ALDRICH, and MAGRATH, a Committee to count the ballots.

The Convention proceeded to ballot for Messenger and Doorkeeper.

On motion of Mr. EDMUND BELLINGER, it was ordered that the election should be decided by a plurality instead of a majority of votes; and the same was ordered.

Messrs. J. V. MARTIN, GLADDEN, and SPAIN, were appointed a committee to count the ballots.

Mr. CUNINGHAM, from the commitee to count the ballots for Clerk of the Convention, reported that JAMES A. STROBHART was duly elected, who immediately entered upon his duties.

Mr. EDMUND BELLINGER, jr., moved the adoption of the following orders :

1. *Ordered,* That the President appoint a Cashier and Assistant Cashier.

2. *Ordered,* That the Clerk act as Reading Clerk, and also superintend such printing as the Convention shall order.

3. *Ordered,* That the reporters for the public journals be allowed access to the Hall, for the purpose of reporting.

4. *Ordered,* That the regular hour of meeting shall be 12 o'clock, m., subject to special orders fixing some other time.

5. *Ordered,* That there be printed for the use of the Convention an Alphabetical List of the names of the members, and also a list of the names arranged according to Congressional and State election divisions.

6. *Ordered,* That the journal of each day's proceedings be printed and laid on the tables of members before the hour of meeting.

The vote was taken upon each separately, and they were agreed to by the Convention.

Mr LAW laid before the Convention the resignation of Hon. GEO. W. DARGAN, a delegate elect from the District of Darlington; which, on motion of Hon. WHITEMARSH B. SEABROOK, was ordered to lie on the table for the present.

Mr. JAMISON offered the following Resolution :

Resolved, That the President appoint a Committee of five members to prepare and report Rules for the government of the Convention.

The resolution was agreed to, and Messrs. JAMISON, BROWN, RHETT, ALDRICH, and HAMILTON, were appointed the Committee.

Mr. EDMUND BELLINGER. jr., offered the following Resolution, which was agreed to :

Resolved, That the proceedings of each day be opened with prayer by such of the clergy as the President shall appoint to perform that appropriate duty.

Mr. JAMISON announced that DONALD ROWE, a delegate elect from Orange Parish, had died since his election; and, in a feeling and impressive manner, commented upon the character of the deceased, and offered the following Resolutions, which were seconded by Hon. B. F. DUNKIN, and were unanimously agreed to:

Resolved, unanimously, That the members of this body have learned with regret the death of DONALD ROWE, a member elect to the Convention.

Resolved, unanimously, That they sincerely mourn his loss, and, in testimony whereof and as a tribute of respect to his memory, they do wear the customary badge of mourning during the session of the Convention.

Resolved, That a copy of the foregoing resolutions be sent by the Secretary of this body to the family of the deceased.

Mr. BURT offered the following Resolution:

Resolved, That a Committee of Five be appointed by the President to make a contract for the printing of the proceedings of this Convention.

The resolution was agreed to, and Messrs. BURT, NANCE, YOUNG, HARLLEE, and BUCHANAN, were appointed the committee.

On motion of Mr. HAMILTON, the Convention, at 3 o'clock, p. m., adjourned until to-morrow, at 12 o'clock, m.

JAMES A. STROBHART,
Clerk of the Convention.

TUESDAY, APRIL 27, 1852.

At 12 o'clock, M., the Convention assembled, pursuant to adjournment, and was called to order by the Clerk.

The roll being called, the President took the Chair.

After prayer by the Rev. DANIEL DUPRE, a delegate from St. James, Santee, the Journal of the previous day was read by the Clerk.

The following additional Delegates appeared at the Clerk's desk, and enrolled their names, viz: N. A. PEAY, of Fairfield; D. St. P. DUBOSE, of Clarendon; A. WHYTE, of York; M. T. APPLEBY, of St. George's, Dorchester; JOHN F. LIVINGSTON, of Abbeville; T. O. ELLIOTT and C. G. MEMMINGER, of St. Philips and St. Michaels; and J. M. DOBY, of Lancaster.

The President then called for reports of Committees.

Mr. J. V. MARTIN, from the Committee to count the votes for Messenger and Doorkeeper, reported B. I. Hayes to have been duly elected to the former, and B. O'Neal to the latter office.

Mr. JAMISON, from the Committee appointed to prepare Rules for the government of the Convention, reported the following:

Rule 1. The President and eighty-four members shall be a quorum to transact business.

2. If any member shall absent himself without leave, he may be sent for at his own expense, and be subject to the censure of the Convention.

3. No member shall speak more than twice to the same point without leave of the Convention.

4. Each member, when speaking, shall address himself to the Chair, standing and uncovered, at his place.

5. If two members rise to speak nearly at the same time, the President shall decide which was first up.

6. Every member, when speaking, shall adhere to the point before the Convention, and shall not be interrupted unless he departs from it, when he may be called to order.

7. When a question of order arises, it shall be decided by the President in the first instance, but any member may appeal from his determination to the Convention.

8. When a motion is made and seconded, it shall, if required by a member, be reduced to writing, and delivered in at the table.

9. When a question is put by the President, and the Convention divides, the Clerk shall, at the request of any seven members present, take down and enter on the Journal the names of all those members who vote for and against the question, and cause them to be published in any gazette of the State.

10. When the President desires to be heard, the members shall take their seats, and keep order whilst he is speaking.

11. When a motion is made for adjournment and seconded, no question shall be debated until the Convention shall have decided that motion.

12. Motions to adjourn, to take a recess, to lay on the table, to postpone indefinitely, or to a day beyond the session, to adjourn a debate, shall be decided without debate, after such short conversations as the President may permit.

13. On points not specified in the above rules, the Convention shall be governed by "the Rules of the House of Representatives of the General Assembly of South Carolina," so far as they are applicable.

All of which were adopted; the 13th Rule having been amended by the slight addition to the last line of the words "so far as they are applicable."

Mr. BURT, from the Committee charged with making a contract for printing the proceedings of the Convention, reported that they had contracted with Messrs. Johnston & Cavis to print for the use of the Convention, on the same terms as like work had been done for the State Senate during the last session of the Legislature, and asked the approval of the Convention. The report was adopted.

A letter from T. G. SIMONS, of St. Philips and St. Michaels, offering his resignation of his seat in the Convention, was read; and, on motion, laid on the table.

The Hon. LANGDON CHEVES submitted the following Resolution:

Resolved, That a Committee of Twenty-one be appointed by the President, to whom shall be referred the act of the General Assembly, entitled "An Act to provide for the appointment of deputies to a Southern Congress, and to call a Convention of the people of this State," with instructions to consider and report thereon.

The resolution was adopted; and, in order that the President might have leisure to select the committee, the Convention, on motion of the Hon. JACOB BOND I'ON, took a recess of one hour. After the expiration of the hour, the Convention re-assembled, and the President announced the following committee, viz:

Messrs. Langdon Cheves, J. P. Richardson, W. B. Seabrook, A. P. Butler, D. E. Huger, R. W. Barnwell, J. J. Evans, J. N. Whitner, D. L. Wardlaw, Edward Frost, F. H. Wardlaw, B. F. Dunkin, J. Buchanan, B. F. Perry, Maxcy Gregg, E. Bellinger, jr , F. W. Pickens, I. W. Hayne, W. W. Harllee, Henry Arthur, Samuel McAliley.

Mr. EDMUND BELLINGER, jr., submitted the following orders for the action of the Convention; and, after consideration, they were adopted:

Ordered, That three hundred copies of the Rules of the Convention be printed for the use of the members.

Ordered, That the Clerk be authorized to furnish stationery for the Convention.

On motion of Mr. CUNINGHAM, the Convention then adjourned until 12 o'clock to-morrow.

JAMES A. STROBHART,
Clerk of the Convention.

WEDNESDAY, APRIL 28, 1852.

At 12 o'clock, M., the Convention assembled, pursuant to adjournment, and was called to order by the Clerk.

The roll being called, and a quorum answering to their names, the President took the Chair.

After prayer by the Rev. J. G. LANDRUM, a delegate from Spartanburg, the journal of the previous day was read by the Clerk. JOHN SCHNIERLE, a delegate from St. Philips and St. Michaels, was announced, appeared at the Clerk's desk, and enrolled his name.

The President then having called for Reports of Committees, and the Chairman of the Committee of Twenty-one having announced that his Committee was not yet ready to submit their Report—

That it might have further time, Mr. LEHRE moved that the Convention adjourn until 12 o'clock, M., to-morrow; which being agreed to, the Convention adjourned accordingly.

JAMES A. STROBHART,
Clerk of the Convention.

THURSDAY, APRIL 29, 1852.

At 12 o'clock, M., the Convention assembled, pursuant to adjournment.

The roll being called, and a quorum having answered to their names, the President took the Chair.

After prayer by the Rev. S. R. ENGLISH, sr., a delegate from Claremont, the journal of the previous day was read.

Reports being in order, the Hon. LANGDON CHEVES, from the Select Committee of Twenty-one, informed the Convention that the Committee was ready to report.

The Report was then read; and on his motion, it was ordered to be printed, and made the special order of the day for to-morrow.

Mr. PERRY, one of the Select Committee of Twenty-one, offered a separate Report of the minority of the same.*

Mr. JOHN BELLINGER moved to amend the majority Report, by adding thereto the following, viz:

"*Be it ordained by this Convention*, That the Legislature of the State shall have the power, by a vote of two-thirds, (accompanied with a notification to the other States,) to withdraw the State of South Carolina from the Federal Union."

Mr. E. BELLINGER, jr., moved that these, together with all other matters connected with the question, be printed with the majority Report; which motion was agreed to.

---

* See Addenda at the end of the Journal.

Mr. GREGG offered a separate Report on his own behalf; which, on his motion, was excepted from the general order, and was ordered to be printed and laid on the table.*

Mr. HARLLEE offered the following Resolution:

Resolved, That the President of the Senate and Speaker of the House of Representatives be invited to seats on this floor.

The Resolution was passed, and the invitation extended by the President.

Under a previous order to that effect, the President announced E. M. WHALEY as Cashier, and O. M. DANTZLER Assistant Cashier, of the Convention.

The Hon. LANGDON CHEVES moved that when the Convention adjourn, it shall stand adjourned until ten o'clock to-morrow.

On motion of Mr. EDMUND BELLINGER, jr., the Convention then adjourned.

JAMES A. STROBHART,
Clerk of the Convention.

FRIDAY, APRIL 30, 1852.

The Convention met, pursuant to adjournment, and the roll was called.

After prayer by the Rev. R. Y. RUSSEL, a Delegate from York, the Clerk read the journal of yesterday.

On motion of Mr. LEHRE, Mr. I. M. DWIGHT, a Delegate from St. Georges, Dorchester, was excused from further attendance on the Convention, on account of illness in his family.

The special order was taken up.

Mr. JOHN BELLINGER addressed the Convention in support of his amendment offered on yesterday, which proposed that it should be ordained by the Convention that the Legislature of the State should have power, by a vote of two-thirds, (accompanied with a notification to the other States,) to withdraw the State of South Carolina from the Federal Union.

The Hon. LANGDON CHEVES moved to lay the amendment on the table.

After a short conversation between the Hon. LANGDON CHEVES, the Hon. A. P. BUTLER and Mr. EDMUND BELLINGER, jr., on this motion,

---

* See Addenda at the end of the Journal.

the yeas and nays were called for by Mr. JOHN BELLINGER, ordered, and taken as follows:

Yeas.--Messrs. Aldrich, Allison, Appleby, Arthur, Barnwell, E. Bellinger, jr., Bethea, Bobo, Bookter, Bouknight, Bradwell, Brockman, Brown, Burt, Butler, Cantey, Caughman, Center, Charles, Cheves, Coit, Cook, Craig, David, Doby, DuBose, P. E. Duncan, B. F. Dunkin, Ellerbe, Elliott, English, J. J. Evans, W. Evans, Farrow, Finley, Frost, Furman, W. Graham, Grimball, Haigler, Hanna, Harllee, Harrison, Hayne, Haynsworth, Higgins, Hope, Huger, I'On, Irby, H. Jones, King, Landrum, Lang, Law, Lehre, Livingston, Magrath, E. Martin, J. C. Martin, R. A. Maxwell, Memminger, Mobley, Moon, McAliley, McBee, Macbeth, McCalla, McCrady, McIlwain, O'Bryan, Patterson, Perrin, Pickens, Poole, Porcher, Pressly, Richardson, Rivers, Rosborough, Russel, Scaife, Schnierle, Seabrook, Sims, Spain, Sumter, Symmes, D. L. Wardlaw, F. H. Wardlaw, Whyte, Whitner, J. Williams, J. H. Williams, W. Williams, Young.—96.

Nays.—His Excellency John H. Means, President; Messrs. Adams, Alston, Atkinson, John Bellinger, E. St. P. Bellinger, Bonham, Buchanan, Cuningham, Dantzler, Davant, DeSaussure, DuPre, Elfe, Frampton, Fripp, Gadberry, Gladden, Gourdin, S. E. Graham, Gregg, Gramling, Hamilton, Henderson, Huguenin, Jamison, Johnson, A. C. Jones, James Jones, Kirk, Latta. Mackay, J. Martin, J. V. Martin, Mason, J. Maxwell, McBride, Nance, Owens, Palmer, Peay, Perry, Read, Rhett, Rice, Ruth, Scott, Toomer, Trapier, Trotti, Vaught, Wallace, Walker, Waring, Whaley, B. H. Wilson, Hugh Wilson, jr., J. D. Williams, Winsmith, Wright.—60.

So the amendment was laid on the table.

Mr. RHETT proposed to amend the ordinance, by declaring and ordaining that the first clause of the second section of the fourth article of the Constitution of the United States, whereby it is provided, that "the citizens of each State shall be entitled to all the privileges and immunities of citizens of the several States," should be rendered null and void within the limits of South Carolina, so far as regards the citizens of Massachusetts and Vermont; and that it should be the duty of the Legislature, by suitable and effectual provisions and penalties, to debar and exclude the citizens of those States from entering, abiding, or holding property within this State, after the ratification of the same.

Mr. RHETT sustained his amendment with much eloquence, and warmly protested against the check to free discussion by motions to lay on the table.

Mr. CUNINGHAM also, in strong and glowing language, joined in this protest.

On motion, Mr. Rhett's amendment was laid on the table.

Mr. ADAMS, as a substitute for the Report of the Committee, offered a resolution, that this Convention, having been called to secede from the Union on account of the past aggressions of the Federal Government, yielding to the popular vote of October last against that remedy, and not agreeing on any other, should now adjourn *sine die.*

Mr. TOOMER offered resolutions recommending to the slave-holding States to call Conventions of the people of their several States, to adopt and carry out measures for the organization of a Southern Confederacy, &c.

Each of these resolutions was, on motion, laid on the table.

The minority report of Mr. PERRY was also, on motion, laid on the table.

Mr. MEMMINGER asked and obtained leave to read a statement of his own opinion and that of those agreeing with him upon the questions under discussion; and moved that it be printed and laid on the table.

The motion to print, meeting with much opposition, was withdrawn by Mr. MEMMINGER. The document was then received and laid on the table.

Mr. HARLLEE then moved the adoption of the report of the Select Committee of Twenty-one, which is as follows:

The Committee of Twenty-one, to whom was referred "An Act to provide for the election of Deputies to a Southern Congress, and the call of a Convention," with instructions to consider and report thereon, respectfully report:

That they have considered the subject referred to them, and have concluded to recommend to the Convention the adoption of the accompanying Resolution and Ordinance:

Resolved by the people of South Carolina in Convention assembled, That the frequent violations of the Constitution of the United States by the Federal Government, and its encroachments upon the reserved rights of the sovereign States of this Union, especially in relation to slavery, amply justify this State, so far as any duty or obligation to her confederates is involved, in dissolving at once all political connection with her co-States; and that she forbears the exercise of this manifest right of self-government from considerations of expediency only.

AN ORDINANCE to declare the right of this State to secede from the Federal Union.

We the People of the State of South Carolina, in Convention assembled, do declare and ordain, and it is hereby declared and ordained, That South Carolina, in the exercise of her sovereign will, as an independent State, acceded to the Federal Union, known as the United States of America; and that in the exercise of the same sovereign will, it is her right, without let, hindrance, or molestation from any power whatsoever, to secede from the said Federal Union; and that for the sufficiency of the causes which may impel her to such separation, she is responsible alone, under God, to the tribunal of public opinion among the nations of the earth.

Upon the motion to adopt the report, the yeas and nays were called for, ordered, and taken as follows:

Yeas.—His Excellency John H. Means, President; Messrs. Aldrich, Allison, Alston, Appleby, Arthur, Atkinson, Barnwell, J. Bellinger, E. Bellinger, jr., E. St. P. Bellinger, Bethea, Bobo, Bonham, Bookter, Bouknight, Bradwell, Brown, Buchanan, Burt, Butler, Cantey, Caughman, Cheves, Coit, Cook, Craig, Cuningham, Dantzler, Davant, David, DeSaussure, Doby, DuBose, B. F. Dunkin, DuPre, Elfe, Ellerbe, Elliott, English, J. J. Evans, W. Evans, Farrow, Finley, Frampton, Frost, Furman, Gadberry, Gladden, S. E. Graham, Gregg, Gramling, Grimball, Haigler, Hanna, Harllee, Harrison, Hayne, Haynsworth, Henderson, Higgins, Hope, Huger, Huguenin, I'On, Irby, Jamison, Johnson, A. C. Jones, James Jones, H. Jones, King, Kirk, Landrum, Lang, Law, Lehre, Livingston, Mackay, Magrath, E. Martin, J. Martin, J. C. Martin, Mason, R. A. Maxwell, J. Maxwell, Memminger, Mobley, Moon, McAliley, Macbeth, McBride, McIlwain, Nance, O'Bryan, Patterson, Peay, Perrin, Pickens, Poole, Porcher, Pressly, Read, Rhett, Rice, Richardson, Rivers, Rosborough, Russel, Ruth, Scaife, Schnierle, Scott, Seabrook, Sims, Spain, Sumter, Symmes, Trapier, Vaught, Wallace, Walker, D. L. Wardlaw, F. H. Wardlaw, Waring, Whaley, B. H. Wilson, Hugh Wilson, jr., Whyte, Whitner, J. Williams, J. D. Williams, J. H. Williams, Winsmith, Wright, Young.—136.

Nays.—Messrs. Adams, Brockman, Center, Charles, P. E. Duncan, Fripp, Gourdin, W. Graham, Hamilton, Latta, J. V. Martin, McBee, McCalla, McCrady, Owens, Palmer, Perry, Toomer, Trotti.—19.

So the report was adopted, and ordered to be engrossed.

On motion of Mr. TROTTI, a Committee of Three were appointed to superintend the engrossing of the resolution and ordinance; and it was ordered that the same be ratified in the usual parliamentary mode, by the signatures of the President and Clerk, and that the great seal of the State be thereunto affixed.

To allow time for engrossing, &c., the Convention then took a recess until five o'clock.

RECESS.

At five o'clock, P. M., the President called the Convention to order.

Mr. ELFE, who by mistake had voted in the negative when the yeas and nays were called on the adoption of the report, was, by consent of the Convention, allowed to change his vote.

On motion of the Hon. A. P. BUTLER, the Clerk of the Convention was allowed five hundred dollars for his regular and extra services.

The Librarian and Keeper of the State House was allowed fifty dollars; the Assistant Clerk of the House of Representatives, the Messenger, and Doorkeeper were allowed each one hundred dollars.

On motion of Mr. BURT, it was ordered that the Treasurer be required to pay the Printers of the Convention such sum as may be due; their accounts to be audited by the Clerk.

Also, that the President of the Convention be authorized to draw his warrant upon the Treasurer for whatever sum may be reported to him, by the Clerk, as due for stationery and other incidental expenses of the Convention.

Also, that a full and minute statement of the expenditures of the Convention, prepared by the Clerk, signed by the President, and attested by the Clerk, be transmitted to the Executive, with a request that the same be laid before the General Assembly, at their next session, for their information.

Also, that five thousand copies of the proceedings of this Convention, and of the report, resolution and ordinance, be printed; and that the same be distributed as follows, under the superintendence of the Clerk:

For the Executive, three hundred copies; for each of our Senators and Representatives in Congress, for their own use, one hundred copies; for each member of this Convention and of the State Legislature, ten copies; and that the remaining copies be for public distribution.

On motion of Mr. E. BELLINGER, jr., it was ordered, that the Clerk do prepare a full index for the journal; and that the journal, together with the resolution and ordinance, and the roll of members, be deposited, *in perpetuam memoriam rei*, amongst the archives of the State.

On motion of Mr. DANTZLER, it was ordered that drafts, signed by the President, and countersigned by the Cashier of the Convention, be issued for the pay of the members, and for such other amounts as shall have been, or may be, ordered by this Convention to be paid.

On motion of Mr. ALDRICH, it was ordered that any delegate who has been excused from attendance on this Convention, for sickness, or other cause, be allowed hereafter to sign the roll of members.

On motion of Mr. BARNWELL, it was resolved, that the President do return the sincere thanks and grateful acknowledgments of this Convention to the Reverend Clergy who have favored us with their prayers. This the President did forthwith, in a very appropriate and feeling manner.

On motion of Mr. E. BELLINGER, jr., the Convention then resolved itself into Committee of the whole, the Hon. J. J. EVANS in the Chair.

The Hon. A. P. BUTLER offered a resolution, tendering the thanks of the Convention to the President, for the very able, dignified, and impartial manner with which he had presided over its deliberations, and for the fidelity and zeal with which he had discharged the onerous and responsible duties of his station.

The resolution was unanimously adopted.

The Committee then rose, and the Chairman reported the resolution, prefaced by a few feeling and very eloquent remarks.

The President, in like spirit and manner, returned his grateful acknowledgments.

The Engrossing Committee reported the resolution and ordinance prepared for ratification. They were then ratified and signed by the President and by the Clerk of the Convention.

On motion of Mr. EDMUND BELLINGER, jr., it was resolved, that when this Convention shall adjourn, it do adjourn *sine die*, AND BE DISSOLVED.

On motion of the Hon. LANGDON CHEVES, it was resolved, that the Convention do now adjourn.

Whereupon, at the hour of half-past six, P. M., of Friday, 30th April, A. D. 1852, the Convention adjourned, and the President announced the Convention DISSOLVED.

ADDENDA

TO THE

JOURNAL OF THE STATE CONVENTION.

MINORITY REPORT BY MR. PERRY.

Mr. PERRY, a member of the Committee of Twenty-one, to whom was referred "An Act to provide for the election of Deputies to a Southern Congress and the call of a Convention," with instructions to consider and report, submitted the following as a minority report, which was read, ordered to be printed, and made the order of the day for to-morrow:

The undersigned, a member of the Committee of Twenty-one, differing from the Committee in their report on the act referred to them, calling this Convention, begs leave to submit the following Preamble and Resolutions, as expressing his views in regard to the important matters contained in said report, and as to the true policy to be pursued by the State of South Carolina in relation to her difficulties with the Federal Government.

APRIL 29, 1852. B. F. PERRY.

Whereas the Legislature of South Carolina, in consequence of the aggressions of Congress and the Northern States on the domestic institutions of the South, deemed it necessary to embody the sovereign power of the State in Convention, in order that the "Commonwealth should suffer no detriment," and for "the purpose of considering the proceedings and recommendations of a Congress of the slave-holding States:" *And whereas* the other slave-holding States have declined meeting South Carolina in a Southern Congress, for the purpose of considering the past aggressions of the Federal Government on an institution in which they all have a common and an equal interest: *And whereas* it would be unwise and imprudent, and wanting in respect to the other Southern States, for South Carolina, under existing circumstances, to take any decisive separate action in a cause which equally belongs to them all: *And whereas* there have been recent manifestations on the part o the Federal Government and a large portion of the Northern people to cease their aggressions on the institutions of the South, and crrry out in good faith the guarantees of the Federal Constitution: *And whereas* a deep-rooted and long-cherished regard for the Union of these States, as "the palladium of our independence," "tranquillity," "peace," "safety," "prosperity," and "liberty," makes it right and proper, honorable and patriotic, that we should "suffer while evils are sufferable," rather "than right ourselves by abolishing the forms to which we have been accustomed :"

Be it therefore resolved, That this Convention will forbear at present to exercise that highest and most sacred of all rights which can belong to a free and brave people—a right secured to them by nature and nature's God, and paramount to all constitutions and political compacts or agreements—the right "to alter or abolish" their government when it becomes destructive of the ends for which it was instituted, and ceases to protect them in the enjoyment of their "lives, liberty, property, and pursuit of happiness."

Resolved, That the Union of the several States of this Confederacy was formed for the purpose of protecting equally the interests of all the States—their domestic institutions, property, and industrial pursuits ; and the existence of African slavery in the Southern States, at the formation of the Federal Union, was not only recognised in the Constitution, but guarantied, and made the basis, in part, of their representation in the Congress of the United States.

Resolved, That this domestic institution of the South is not only moral and correct in the opinion of this Convention, but a great blessing to the African race; and absolutely necessary for the continued peace and prosperity of the slave-holding States; and as such will be forever defended and maintained by them at any and all hazards, and to the last extremity of their existence as a people.

Resolved, That South Carolina, through her sovereign Convention, now pledges herself to her sister Southern States, to resist, in company with them, or alone if need be, by all the means which nature and God have given her, any and every attempt on the part of Congress to interfere with slavery in the States, or the slave trade between the States, or to abolish slavery in the District of Columbia without the consent of the owners, or to exclude slavery from the Southern territories of the United States, or the forts, navy yards, and other public places in the slave-holding States belonging to the Federal Government, or refuse the admission of a State into the Union on account of slavery, or refuse to enforce and carry out the existing constitutional provisions on the subject of rendition of fugitive slaves, or alter or change the Federal Constitution in any respect touching slavery.

REPORT OF MR. GREGG.

Mr. GREGG, from the same Committee, submitted a report on his own behalf, stating his reasons for not concurring in the report of the Committee, which, on his motion, was laid on the table, and ordered to be printed.

The undersigned, a member of the Convention, to which was referred for consideration the Act of the General Assembly calling together this Convention, being dissatisfied with the Report of the Committee, not on account of what is contained in it, but of what is omitted, respectfully asks leave to state his reasons.

The position of South Carolina at this time is a most difficult and embarrassing one. Suffering under injuries which render a continuance in the present Union incompatible with honor or safety; but deserted by other States, suffering under the same injuries, and whose solemn pledges of resistance gave South Carolina a right to expect very different action from them;—the citizens of the State became divided in opinion as to the course proper to be taken. One portion of them believed that all hope being lost of any other States seceding from the Confederacy by a concerted movement, it was necessary for South Carolina to vindicate herself from intolerable wrongs by seceding alone. Another portion regarded this course as unwise, and thought it necessary to wait for the support of other States. The prospect of such support has grown fainter day by day, until it has receded to an indefinite distance; and that portion of our citizens who have placed their only hope in it, now find themselves powerless to effect their object. But by the popular majority which they have exhibited, opposed to exercising the right of secession at this time, they have also paralyzed the power of their fellow-citizens who desired to adopt that course.

Under these circumstances this Convention meets, charged with the duty of seeing that the Commonwealth receive no detriment. To secede under such circumstances is impracticable. To obtain the aid of any other State in resisting the aggressions which have been committed by the Northern States and the Federal Government is hopeless. Unless some effective mode of action could be adopted, which, while stopping short of secession, might place and preserve the State in a position of readiness to take advantage of the earliest opportunity for successful resistance, guarding, as far as practicable, in the mean time, against the many corrupting influences of a longer connection with the Government which oppresses us, nothing remains but submission—a submission likely to be fatal If any such mode of action could be devised and proposed by those who are opposed to separate secession, it would beyond doubt be accepted and supported by those who have been in favor of that measure.

The Report of the Committee is unsatisfactory to the undersigned, because it contains no recommendation of any action whatever beyond a mere declaration of the right of secession, and of the injuries which have been suffered, justifying its exercise by South Carolina.

If a protestation in favor of our rights, made at a time when in fact we are deprived of them, can be of any avail towards preserving them in recollection and recovering them at a future day, it is wise and proper to make such protestation. But actions outweigh words, and one step in advance towards practical resistance would be worth more than the strongest declarations. If the majority of the Committee had devised any measures with a character of practical resistance, however moderate, impressed upon them, the undersigned would have greatly preferred, for the sake of that harmony which is of such high importance if ever the State is to be rescued from its present condition, to acquiesce in their Report. He believes that such measures might be devised by those who have opposed separate secession, and that, if adopted with unanimity by the people of the State, they would afford some reasonable hope of ultimate deliverance. But seeing no prospect that the introduction of any such measures under present circumstances, and against the determined opposition of those who have defeated secession, could result in any good to the State, he has, as a member of the Committee, nothing to recommend. He is willing to vote for the declaration of principles contained in the Resolution and accompanying Ordinance ; but he desires at the same time to leave on the record of the proceedings of this Convention his distinct declaration, that it is not in accordance with his wishes that nothing more hould be done to prevent detriment to the Commonwealth.

MAXCY GREGG.

ALPHABETICAL LIST

OF

MEMBERS OF THE STATE CONVENTION,

ELECTED IN FEBRUARY, 1851.

JOHN H. MEANS, PRESIDENT, FAIRFIELD.

ADAMS, JAMES U., *Richland.*
ALDRICH, A. P., *Barnwell.*
ALLISON, R. T., *York.*
ALSTON, T. P., *All Saints'.*
APPLEBY, M. T., *St. George's, Dorchester.*
ARTHUR, HENRY, *Lexington.*
ATKINSON, SAMUEL T., *P. George, Winyaw.*
BARNWELL, R. W., *St. Phillips and St. Michael's.*
BEATY, JAMES, *Horry.*
BELLINGER, JOHN, *St. Phillips and St. Michael's.*
BELLINGER, EDMUND, Jr., *Barnwell.*
BELLINGER, E. St. P., *St. Bartholomew's.*
BETHEA, JOHN C., *Marion.*
BOBO, W. J., *Union.*
BONHAM, M. L., *Edgefield.*
BOOKTER, CHRISTIAN, *Richland.*
BOUKNIGHT, R. B., *Edgefield.*
BRADWELL, ISAAC, jr., *St. James', Goose Creek.*
BROCKMAN, T. P., *Greenville.*
BROWN, A. H., *St. Andrew's.*
BUCHANAN, J., *Fairfield.*
BURT, F., *Pendleton.*
BUTLER, A. P., *St. Phillips and St. Michael's.*
CANTEY, JOHN, *Kershaw.*
CAUGHMAN, H. J., *Lexington.*
CENTER, JESSE, *Greenville.*
CHARLES, E. W., *Darlington.*
CHEVES LANGDON, *St. Phillips and St. Michael's.*
COIT, J. C., *Chesterfield.*

COOK, W. J., *Darlington.*
CRAIG, HUGH, *Chesterfield.*
CUNINGHAM, JOHN, *St Phillips and St. Michael's.*
DANTZLER, O. M., *St. Matthew's.*
DARGAN, GEO. W., *Darlington.*
DAVANT, R. J., *St. Luke's.*
DAVID, J. E., *Marlboro.*
DeSAUSSURE, W. F., *Richland.*
DOBY, J. M., *Lancaster.*
DOZIER, A. W., *Williamsburg.*
DuBOSE, D. St. P., *Clarendon.*
DUNCAN, P. E., *Greenville.*
DUNKIN, B. F., *St. Phillips and St. Michael's.*
DuPRE, DANIEL, *St. James', Santee.*
DWIGHT, I. M., *St. George's, Dorchester.*
ELFE, GEORGE, *St. Thomas and St. Dennis'.*
ELLERBE, W. T., *Marlboro.*
ELLIOTT, T. O., *St. Phillips and St. Michael's.*
ENGLISH, T. R., sen., *Claremont.*
EVANS, J. J., *Darlington.*
EVANS, W., *Marion.*
FARROW, JAMES, *Spartanburg.*
FINLEY, W. P., *St. Phillips and St. Michael's.*
FRAMPTON, JOHN E., *Prince William's.*
FRIPP, JOHN, *St. Helena.*
FROST, EDWARD, *St. Phillips and St. Michael's.*
FURMAN, C. M., *St. Phillips and St. Michael's.*
GADBERRY, J. M., *Union.*
GLADDEN, A. H., *Richland.*
GOURDIN, THEO. L., *St. Stephen's.*
GRAHAM, SAMUEL E., *Williamsburg.*
GRAHAM, W., *Barnwell.*
GREGG, MAXCY, *Richland.*
GRAMLING, M., *Orange.*
GRIMBALL, J. B., *St. Paul's.*
HAIGLER, H. A., *St. Matthew's.*
HAMILTON, D. H., *St. Peter's.*
HANNA, W. J., *Chesterfield.*
HARLLEE, W. W., *Marion.*
HARRISON, WILEY, *Edgefield.*
HAYNE, I. W., *St. Phillips and St. Michael's.*
HAYNSWORTH, W., *Claremont.*

HENDERSON, D. S., *St. Bartholomew's.*
HIGGINS, F. B., *Newberry.*
HOPE, J. C., *Lexington.*
HUGER, D. E., *St Phillips and St. Michael's.*
HUGUENIN, J. G., *St. Luke's.*
HUNTER, W., *Pendleton.*
I'ON, JACOB B., *Christ Church.*
IRBY, JAMES H., *Laurens.*
JAMISON, D. F., *Orange.*
JOHNSON, W. R., *Marion.*
JONES, A. C., *Laurens.*
JONES, JAMES, *Edgefield.*
JONES, HARTFORD, *Horry.*
KING, M., *St. Phillips and St. Michael's.*
KIRK, P. C., *St. John's, Berkley.*
LAKE, J. A., *Edgefield.*
LANDRUM, J. G., *Spartanburg.*
LANG, THOMAS, *Kershaw.*
LATTA, W. A., *York.*
LAW, E. A., *Darlington.*
LEHRE, THOMAS, *St. Phillips and St. Michael's.*
LIVINGSTON, J. F., *Abbeville.*
MACKAY, GEO. C., *Prince William's.*
MAGRATH, A. G., *St. Phillips and St. Michael's.*
MARTIN, EDMUND, *St. Peter's.*
MARTIN, J., *Pendleton.*
MARTIN, J. C., *Abbeville.*
MARTIN, J. V., *Barnwell.*
MASON, D. M., *Williamsburg.*
MAXWELL, R. A., *Pendleton.*
MAXWELL, JOHN, *Pendleton.*
MEMMINGER, C. G., *St. Phillips and St. Michael's.*
MOBLEY, ISAIAH, *Chester.*
MOON, PETER, *Newberry.*
MOORE, J. S., *York.*
McALILEY, SAMUEL, *Chester.*
McBEE, V., *Greenville.*
MACBETH, C., *St. Phillips and St. Michael's.*
McBRIDE, B., *Prince William's.*
McCALLA, G., *Abbeville.*
McCRADY, E., *St. Phillips and St. Michael's.*
McILWAIN, J. D., *Lancaster.*

NANCE, DAYTON, *Newberry.*
O'BRYAN, L., *St. Bartholomew's.*
O'HEAR, J. S., *St. Thomas and St. Dennis.*
OWENS, W. A., *Fairfield.*
PALMER, S. J., *St. James', Santee.*
PATTERSON, L. J., *Kershaw*
PEAY, N. A., *Fairfield.*
PERRIN, THOS. C., *Abbeville.*
PERRY, B. F., *Greenville.*
PICKENS, F. W., *Edgefield.*
POOLE, R. C., *Spartanburg.*
PORCHER, W. MAZYCK, *St. Stephen's.*
PRESSLY, G. W., *Abbeville.*
READ, J. H., sr., *Prince George, Winyaw.*
RHETT, EDMUND, *St. Helena.*
RICE, B. H., *Union.*
RICHARDSON, J P., *Clarendon.*
RIVERS, JOHN, *St. Andrew's.*
ROSBOROUGH, W. A., *Chester.*
RUSSEL, R. Y., *York.*
RUTH, A. M., *St. Peter's.*
SCAIFE, C. T., *Chester.*
SCHNIERLE, JOHN, *St. Phillips and St. Michael's*
SCOTT, E. B., *St. Paul's.*
SEABROOK, W. B., *St. John's, Colleton.*
SIMONS, T. G., *St. Phillips and St. Michael's.*
SIMS, J. S., *Union.*
SLOAN, WM., *Pendleton.*
SPAIN, A. C., *Claremont.*
SUMTER, F., *Claremont.*
SYMMES, F. W., *Pendleton.*
TOOMER, A. V., *Christ Church.*
TRAPIER, J. H., *Prince George's, Dorchester.*
TROTTI, S. W., *Barnwell.*
VAUGHT, PETER, *All Saints'.*
VERNON, J. J., *Spartanburg.*
WALLACE, P. M., *Spartanburg.*
WALKER DAVID,*St. Bartholomew's.*
WARDLAW, D. L., *Abbeville.*
WARDLAW, F. H., *Edgefield.*
WARING, M., *St. John's, Berkley.*
WHALEY, E. M., *St. John's, Colleton,*

WILSON, B. H., *Prince George, Winyaw.*
WILSON, HUGH, jr., *St. John's, Colleton.*
WHYTE, A., *York.*
WHITNER, J. N., *Pendleton.*
WILLIAMS, JOHN, *Lancaster.*
WILLIAMS, J. D., *Laurens.*
WILLIAMS, J. H., *Newberry.*
WILLIAMS, W., *St. James', Goose Creek.*
WINSMITH, JOHN, *Spartanburg.*
WITHERSPOON, S. W., *Clarendon.*
WRIGHT, THOMAS, *Laurens.*
YOUNG, H. C., *Laurens.*

MEMBERS OF THE STATE CONVENTION.

ARRANGED ACCORDING TO CONGRESSIONAL DISTRICTS.

FIRST.

DISTRICTS.	NAMES.	PARISHES.
Spartanburg	JAMES FARROW, J. G. LANDRUM, R. C. POOLE, J. J. VERNON, P. M. WALLACE, JOHN WINSMITH.	
Union	W. J. BOBO, J. M. GADBERRY, B. H. RICE, J. S. SIMS.	
York	R. T. ALLISON, W. A. LATTA, J. S. MOORE, R. Y. RUSSEL, A. WHYTE.	
Chester	ISAIAH MOBLEY, SAMUEL McALILEY, W. A. ROSBOROUGH, C. T. SCAIFE.	

SECOND.

DISTRICTS.	NAMES.	PARISHES.
Pendleton *Pickens & Anderson*	J. N. WHITNER, F. W. SYMMES, WM. SLOAN, JOHN MAXWELL, R. A. MAXWELL, J. MARTIN, W. HUNTER, F. BURT,	
Greenville	JESSE CENTER, B. F. PERRY, V. McBEE, P. E. DUNCAN, T. P. BROCKMAN.	
Laurens	H. C. YOUNG, THOMAS WRIGHT, J. D. WILLIAMS, A. C. JONES, JAMES H. IRBY.	

THIRD.

DISTRICTS.		NAMES.	PARISHES.
Lancaster		J. M. DOBY, J. D. McILWAIN, JOHN WILLIAMS.	
Kershaw		JOHN CANTEY, THOS. LANG, L. J. PATTERSON.	
Fairfield		J. BUCHANAN, J. H. MEANS, W. A. OWENS, N. A. PEAY.	
Richland		JAMES U. ADAMS, C. BOOKTER, W. F. DESAUSSURE, MAXCY GREGG, A. H. GLADDEN.	
Sumter	*Clarendon.*	D. ST. P. DUBOSE, J. P. RICHARDSON, S. W. WITHERSPOON.	
Sumter	*Claremont.*	T. R. ENGLISH, sr., W. HAYNSWORTH, A. C. SPAIN, F. SUMTER.	

FOURTH.

DISTRICTS.	NAMES.	PARISHES.
Chesterfield	J. C. COIT, HUGH CRAIG, W. J. HANNA.	
Marlborough	J. E. DAVID, W. T. ELLERBE, W. J. COOK.	
Darlington	E. A. LAW, J. J. EVANS, G. W. DARGAN, E. W. CHARLES.	
Marion	W. R. JOHNSON, W. W. HARLLEE, W. EVANS, JOHN C. BETHEA,	
Horry	HARTFORD JONES, JAMES BEATY.	
Georgetown	B. H. WILSON, J. H. READ, sr. J. H. TRAPIER, S. T. ATKINSON.	*P. G. Winyaw.*
Georgetown	PETER VAUGHT, T. P. ALSTON.	*All Saints.*
Williamsburg	A. W. DOZIER, SAMUEL E. GRAHAM. D. M. MASON.	

FIFTH.

DISTRICTS.	NAMES.	PARISHES.
Abbeville	J. C. MARTIN, D. L. WARDLAW, G. W. PRESSLY, G. McCALLA, THOS. C. PERRIN, J. F. LIVINGSTON.	
Newberry	F. B. HIGGINS, PETER MOON, DRAYTON NANCE, J. H. WILLIAMS,	
Edgefield	J. JONES, F. H. WARDLAW, M. L. BONHAM, WILEY HARRISON, J. A. LAKE, F. W. PICKENS, R. B. BOUKNIGHT,	
Lexington	HENRY ARTHUR, J. C. HOPE, H. J. CAUGHMAN.	

SIXTH.

DISTRICTS.	NAMES.	PARISHES.
Charleston	R. W. BARNWELL, JOHN BELLINGER, A. P. BUTLER, LANGDON CHEVES, J. CUNINGHAM, B. F. DUNKIN, T. O. ELLIOTT, W. P. FINLEY, EDWD. FROST, C. M. FURMAN, I. W. HAYNE, D. E. HUGER, M. KING, THOS. LEHRE, A. G. MAGRATH, C. G. MEMMINGER, C. MACBETH, E. McCREADY, JOHN SCHNIERLE, T. G. SIMONS.	*St. Philips and St. Michaels.*
	S. J. PALMER, DANL. DuPRE.	*St. James, Santee.*

SIXTH.

DISTRICTS.	NAMES.	PARISHES.
Charleston—continued...	W. M. PORCHER, T. L. GOURDIN.	*St. Stephens.*
	GEO. ELFE, J. S. O'HEAR.	*St. Thomas and St Dennis.*
	ISAAC BRADWELL, jr. W. WILLIAMS.	*St. James, Goose Creek.*
	P. C. KIRK, MORTON WARING.	*St. Johns, Berkley.*
	JACOB BOND I'ON, A. V. TOOMER.	*Christ Church.*
	JOHN RIVERS, A. H. BROWN.	*St. Andrews.*

SEVENTH.

DISTRICTS.	NAMES.	PARISHES.
Orangeburg...........	D. F. JAMISON, M. GRAMLING.	*Orange.*
	O. M. DANTZLER, H. A. HAIGLER.	*St. Mathews.*
Barnwell..............	E. BELLINGER, Jr., S. W. TROTTI, J. V. MARTIN, A. P. ALDRICH, W. GRAHAM.	
Colleton..............	DAVID WALKER, D. S HENDERSON, L. O'BRYAN, E. S. P. BELLINGER.	*St Bartholomews*
	M. T. APPLEBY, I. M. DWIGHT.	*St. Georges, Dorchester.*
	W. B. SEABROOK, HUGH WILSON, Jr., E. M. WHALEY.	*St Johns', Colleton,*
	J. B. GRIMBALL, E. B. SCOTT,	*St. Pauls.*
Beaufort..............	G. C. MACKAY, B. McBRIDE, J. E. FRAMPTON.	*Prince Williams.*
	EDMUND RHETT, JOHN FRIPP.	*St. Helena.*
	D. H. HAMILTON, A. M. RUTH, EDMUND MARTIN.	*St. Peter's.*
	J. G. HUGUENIN, R. J. DAVANT.	*St. Luke.*

ACTS OF THE GENERAL ASSEMBLY

RELATIVE TO

THE STATE CONVENTION.

AN ACT to provide for the appointment of Deputies to a Southern Congress, and to call a Convention of the People of this State.

Whereas the Convention of the slave-holding States lately assembled at Nashville have recommended to the said States to meet in Congress or Convention, to be held at such time and place as the States desiring to be represented may designate, to be composed of double the number of their Senators and Representatives in the Congress of the United States, entrusted with full power and authority to deliberate, with the view and intention of arresting further aggressions, and if possible of restoring the constitutional rights of the South, and if not, to recommend due provision for their future safety and independence :

I. *Be it enacted by the Senate and House of Representatives now met and sitting in General Assembly, and by the authority of the same,* That eighteen Deputies shall be appointed in the manner hereinafter provided, who are hereby authorized, as Deputies from the State, to meet such Deputies as may be appointed and authorized by any other slave-holding State in Congress or Convention, as above recommended, and to join with them in discussing and devising such measures as, in their opinion, may be adequate to obtain the objects proposed by the said Convention at Nashville, and in reporting such measures to the said several slave-holding States, as, when agreed to and fully confirmed by them, or any of them, will effectually provide for the same.

II. Four of the said Deputies shall be elected by joint ballot of the General Assembly at its present session ; and the qualified voters in each Congressional District in this State shall elect two, at such time as is hereinafter prescribed.

III. The Governor of this State shall issue writs of election to the Managers of Election, requiring them to hold elections in their respective Congressional Districts, on the second Monday in October next, and the day following, for two Deputies to the said Congress, in each Congressional District, and the said Managers shall thereupon advertise and hold such elections, and make due return thereof to the Governor.

IV. That the Governor shall duly commission all the said Deputies, so to be elected by the General Assembly and by the people; and shall, in concert with the Governor or other proper authorities of other States joining in such Congress, appoint the time and place of meeting, and give due notice thereof; and any of the Deputies on the part of this State who may attend at such time and place, shall have full power to represent the State, as hereinbefore provided.

V. That a Convention of the people of the State of South Carolina is hereby ordained, to be assembled in the Town of Columbia, as hereinafter provided, for the purpose, in the first place, of taking into consideration the proceedings and recommendations of a Congress of the slave-holding States, if the same shall meet and be held; and for the further purpose of taking into consideration the general welfare of this State, in view of her relations to the Laws and Government of the United States, and thereupon to take care that the Commonwealth of South Carolina shall suffer no detriment.

VI. That on the second Monday in February next, and on the day following, the Managers of Elections for the several Districts in this State, shall, after giving public notice, as in cases of elections for Members of the Legislature, open the polls and hold elections in their respective Districts for Delegates to the said Convention, in all respects in the same manner and form, and at the same places, as elections are now conducted for Members of the Legislature: And all persons who are qualified and entitled, by the Constitution and Laws of this State, to vote for Members of the Legislature, shall be qualified and entitled to vote for said Delegates to said Convention; and, in case of any vacancy occurring by death, resignation, or removal from the State, or refusal to serve, of any person elected a Delegate to the said Convention the presiding officer of the said Convention shall issue his writ authorizing and requiring the Managers of Elections, in the election districts in which such vacancy may have occurred, after giving due notice thereof, to open a poll and hold an election to fill such vacancy, as in cases for the election of Members of the Legislature.

VII. That each election district throughout the State shall be entitled to elect and send to the said Convention, a number of Delegates equal to the whole number of Senators and Representatives which such District is now entitled to send to the Legislature; and the Delegates to the said Convention shall be entitled to the same freedom of arrest in going to, returning from, and whilst in attendance on, said Convention, as is extended to the Members of the Legislature.

VIII. That all free white male citizens of this State, of the age of twenty-one years and upwards, shall be eligible to a seat in said Convention.

IX. That the Governor be, and is hereby requested, forthwith, after the passage of this Act, to communicate an authentic copy of the same to the

Executives of each of the slave-holding States of the Union, and to urge upon the said authorities, in such manner as he may deem best, the desire of the State of South Carolina, that the said slave-holding States do send duly commissioned Deputies to meet the Deputies herein provided, to be elected, at the city of Montgomery, in the State of Alabama, on the second day of January, Anno Domini, one thousand eight hundred and fifty-two.

X. That it shall be the duty of his Excellency the Governor of the State, by his proclamation, to call together said Convention, and appoint the time for the meeting thereof, whenever, at any period before the next Session of this General Assembly, the conjuncture of a Southern Congress, contemplated in the purpose of this Act, shall have happened. *Provided*, That in case the Governor shall not assemble the Convention anterior to the next Session of this Legislature, this General Assembly shall, by a majority of votes, fix the time for the meeting of said Convention.

XI. That the said Convention may be continued by adjournment from time to time, so long as may be necessary for the purposes aforesaid; *Provided, however*, That unless sooner dissolved by their own authority, the said Convention shall cease and determine in twelve months from the day on which the said Convention shall first assemble.

In the Senate House, the twentieth day of December, in the year of our Lord one thousand eight hundred and fifty, and in the seventy-fifth year of the Sovereignty and Independence of the United States of America.

ROBERT F. W. ALLSTON,
President of the Senate.
JAMES SIMONS,
Speaker House of Representatives.

AN ACT to fix the time for the meeting of the Convention, elected under the authority of an Act, entitled "An Act to provide for the appointment of Deputies to a Southern Congress, and to call a Convention of the people of this State," passed in the year of our Lord one thousand eight hundred and fifty.

Be it enacted by the Senate and House of Representatives, now met and sitting in General Assembly, and by the authority of the same, That the fourth Monday in April next, be, and the same is hereby, fixed as the time for the assembling of the Convention of the people of this State, provided for and elected under the authority of an Act, entitled "An Act to provide for the appointment of Deputies to a Southern Congress, and to call a Convention of the people of this State," passed on the twentieth day of December, in the year of our Lord one thousand eight hundred and fifty.

In the Senate House, the sixteenth day of December, in the year of our Lord one thousand eight hundred and fifty-one, and in the seventy-sixth year of the Sovereignty and Independence of the United States of America.

ROBERT F. W. ALLSTON,
President of the Senate.
JAMES SIMONS,
Speaker House of Representatives.

EXTRACT FROM AN ACT, *entitled "An Act to make appropriations for the year commencing in October, one thousand eight hundred and fifty-one."*

For the pay of the Members of the State Convention, to be held on the fourth Monday in April next, ten thousand dollars, if so much be necessary; each member to receive the same pay that is now by law allowed to Members of the Legislature; for the Clerk, and the Messenger and the Doorkeeper of the said Convention, each the same pay that is now by law allowed to the Members of the Legislature.

In the Senate House, the sixteenth day of December, in the year of our Lord one thousand eight hundred and fifty-one, and in the seventy-sixth year of the Sovereignty and Independence of the United States of America.

ROBERT F. W. ALLSTON,
President of the Senate.
JAMES SIMONS,
Speaker House of Representatives.

A JOINT RESOLUTION of the Legislature, granting the use of the Hall of the House of Representatives to the State Convention.

Resolved, That the use of the State House and of the Legislative Library be, and the same are hereby, tendered to the Convention of the State, appointed by an Act of the General Assembly, to convene in the town of Columbia, on the fourth Monday in April, 1852, and that the Keeper of the State House and Librarian are hereby directed to be in attendance on said Convention.

In the House of Representatives, December 15, 1851.

Resolved, That the House do agree to the Resolution.

Ordered, That it be sent to the Senate for concurrence.

By order,

T. W. GLOVER, C. H. R.

In the Senate, December 15, 1851.

Resolved, That the Senate do concur in the Resolution.

Ordered, That it be returned to the House of Representatives.

By order,

W. E. MARTIN, C. S.

INDEX

TO THE

JOURNAL OF THE STATE CONVENTION.

O

P

R

www.ingramcontent.com/pod-product-compliance
Lightning Source LLC
LaVergne TN
LVHW011121110826
845150LV00008B/2212
* 9 7 8 1 4 1 8 1 9 7 8 7 2 *